The Un[it Trust] Handbook

A Step-by-Step Comprehensive Blueprint to Investing in Unit Trusts for Beginners

Introduction

So, you want to invest in unit trusts? You've heard they are great investment vehicles; they have wonderfully diversified portfolios, and you don't even have to choose the assets and equities.

All you need to do is to invest your money and wait for the gains. All this makes them unique and amazing investments, no?

Yes, it does. And yes, all of the above is true about unit trusts. But there is a lot more you need to know about them.

Mind you, you don't need to know a lot before investing in unit trusts since they are so straightforward, but you will be much better placed than your counterparts if you take the time to learn about them. At the very least, you can determine which of your prospective unit trust options suits you best.

This guide will walk you through every facet of unit trusts, from what they are to how they work, the various ways you can invest in them, the costs involved, and much more.

PS: I'd like your feedback. If you are happy with this book, please leave a review on Amazon.

Please leave a review for this book on Amazon by visiting the page below:

https://amzn.to/2VMR5qr

Table of Content

Introduction ———————— 2

Chapter 1: A Comprehensive Overview of Unit Trusts ——— 8

What is a Unit Trust? ————— 9

What are the Similarities Between Unit Trusts and Mutual Funds? ___11

What are the Differences Between Unit Trusts and Mutual Funds? ——— 13

Putting Together a UIT Portfolio __ 14

What are the Prevalent Advantages of Investing in Unit Trusts? ———— 18

What are the Disadvantages Involved in Investing in Unit Trusts? ——— 23

Who are Unit Trusts Most Suitable for? ———————————— 30

Chapter 2: Understanding How Unit Trusts Work & Their Profitability _____38

How Do Investors Make Gains/Losses in Unit Trusts? _____ 40

How Much Could You Lose? _____ 42

How Does a Unit Trust's Performance Work? _____ 43

How are Unit Trusts Priced? _____ 45

What are the Different Unit Classes? 49

Chapter 3: The Different Ways of Investing in a Unit Trust_____58

The Different Ways You Can Invest in a Unit Trust _____ 58

What is FICA & Why Is It Relevant? 62

How Much Should You Invest in a Unit Trust? _____ 65

Is a Debit Order a Smarter Choice than a Lump Sum Investment and Vice Versa? _____ 66

Chapter 4: All About Unit Trust Assets, Risk, Returns, and Volatility _____ 69

What are the Different Asset Classes, and How Do They Produce Returns? 70

A Guide to Understanding Risk, Return & Volatility in Unit Investment Trusts _____ 77

Why is It So Vital that Your Returns Trump Inflation? _____ 90

Chapter 5: A Comprehensive Guide on the Costs Involved in Investing in Unit Trusts _____ 92

Are Unit Investment Trusts Taxable? _____ 100

How is Income Tax Paid on Unit Trusts? _____ 100

Conclusion _____ 108

Chapter 1: A Comprehensive Overview of Unit Trusts

"Do not put all your eggs in one basket."

This age-old proverb summarizes the concept of diversification in investment. In this context, it points to investors minimizing/managing risk in their portfolios by having their investments spread across and within multiple asset classes.

There is no shortage of choices regarding financial vehicles offering diversification. Unit investment trusts, or unit trusts, are one of those options.

Unit investment trusts, abbreviated as UITs, are in the same category as mutual funds. They are different assets; however, many investors think they are the same.

UITs have multiple similarities to mutual funds, including that both pool monies from multiple investors, and the pooled monies hold securities such as bonds. However, they also have marked differences; we will look at all this in this chapter.

But first, let's delve deeper into defining a unit of trust.

What is a Unit Trust?

UITs raise funds by selling shares to investors, known as "units." Each unit represents a slice of ownership and gives each investor a proportional "right to income" and capital gains generated by the fund's investments. These investments are typically either bonds or stocks.

Unit trusts are usually only ever issued once/at one point in time, and after raising the intended funding, they are promptly closed, and new investors cannot join.

Unit trusts are mandated to have a Trust/Fund Manager, a Trustee, and a Custodian, per the Rules. The trust manager, also called an asset manager, administers, manages, and ensures that investments made using client money align with the fund's objectives. These are effectively the custodians of unit trusts. They draw up the investment paths of the fund. They determine its goals and objectives, decide which investments to pursue, and manage the fund. They collect an investment management fee, a fixed, upfront fee from the investor. You must pay this fee regardless of how well or badly the fund performs.

A company, typically a bank, is designated as a custodian by the investment Authority to hold/keep the funds and securities of pooled investment schemes or unit trust in trust. On the other hand, trustees ensure that the investors' interests are always protected.

What are the Similarities Between Unit Trusts and Mutual Funds?

We pointed out that UITs are quite similar to mutual funds.

Here are the primary similarities between both:

1. Both UITs and mutual funds pool monies from multiple investors and then invest based on the particular investment goals of the fund.

2. Like mutual funds, UITs can be purchased and sold anytime during the day. However, both are only priced once daily, meaning that units are assigned only one price each day, and this price will not fluctuate until the end of the trading day.

Compare this to investing directly in shares in the stock market, where share prices may fluctuate throughout the trading day, sometimes from one minute to the next.

3. Another similarity is that both are designed for long-term investing. They are unwise investment options if you want a quick ROI or to get your money back as fast as possible. We'll examine this salient trait as the guide goes deeper into investing in these funds.

What are the Differences Between Unit Trusts and Mutual Funds?

There are key differences between these quite similar investment vehicles:

1. For starters, once a UIT has its portfolio set, it generally stays the same for the fund's entire life until the maturation/termination date, except for major corporate happenings, such as mergers or bankruptcy proceedings.

   Mutual fund portfolios, on the other hand, do not have to stay the same and are more flexible. Changes in the portfolio can be activated should the asset manager(s) decide it is the way to go, and, at times, entire overhauls of their portfolios.

2. Another difference is that UITs, unlike mutual funds, have a maturation or

termination date. Once this date arrives, they promptly expire and become invalid. The latter, in comparison, can exist in perpetuity.

Moving on:

The fund's fact sheet and prospectus documents outline the investment goals of each specific fund.

Here is [an example of a fact sheet and prospectus documents](https://efaidnbmnnnibpcajpcglclefindmkaj/https://www.eunittrust.com.my/pdf/Factsheets/040003082019_fs.pdf)[1].

Putting Together a UIT Portfolio

Concerning investment goals and objectives, some funds focus on attaining sizable capital growth in the least amount of time possible. In

---

[1] https://efaidnbmnnnibpcajpcglclefindmkaj/https://www.eunittrust.com.my/pdf/Factsheets/040003082019_fs.pdf

contrast, others favor generating steady, recurrent income over capital growth.

Unit trusts have diversified portfolios, as we have already pointed out. They invest their investor's money in various investment securities, with most of their investments being either bonds or stocks, or a mix of the two.

While most funds are similar in that they limit their investments to stocks and bonds, with some opting for a mix of both, they differ, from one fund to the next, regarding the particular markets they invest in.

Some focus on developing more niche markets, such as developing Asian/Eastern European growth markets, which are still largely in their teething stage, and thus have a narrower operation mandate. But with the lower mandate comes the potential for huge rewards and great spikes in capital growth. This is because these markets are still young and have great growth potential.

However, there is also great risk involved since these markets are not quite as established as the larger ones are. This could make them less steady and considerably more volatile, making it much easier to lose the funding capital and have difficulty getting steady income on the investments. These markets present a high-risk, high-reward prospect. When it pays off, the returns can be very handsome.

Other funds invest in stocks and bonds in investment powerhouse countries such as the United States, Japan, or China and, as such, have a much larger mandate. The risk of investing in these markets is low, and the rewards are also on the lower side.

Individual funds also can specialize in certain investment themes; for instance, some funds specialize purely in industries like healthcare entities, while others will primarily invest in tech companies.

If your risk tolerance is high and you have no issues taking a huge leap to get huge rewards, then funds that invest in developing markets may interest you. If you're cagier with your money and want almost-guaranteed income, you may want to choose funds that invest in larger markets and have a larger mandate.

Let's now look at the advantages that come with investing in UITs.

What are the Prevalent Advantages of Investing in Unit Trusts?

Here are the most prevalent advantages when it comes to unit trusts.

1) Simple & transparent

You don't need considerable time, knowledge, or experience to invest in a unit trust.

A fund's track record, historical returns, and investment holdings are all clear in its concise fact sheet, making it possible to make an informed decision about whether it is a good investment for you without needing to be seasoned at investing.

2) High liquidity

Although they are often not public, UITs, still have a high level of liquidity. You can typically enter/exit your investment on any particular business day, as you can with stocks, except for weekends and past trading hours (5 pm to 8 am).

When choosing whether to purchase or sell your unit trust, you may accept the unit price at the trading day's closing time or wait until the next day to see if it climbs.

3) Low initial amount of investment

Typically, $500 is the minimum investment amount you will need to join a UIT. These trusts, where individual investors pool their monies, are called retail funds.

As for institutional funds, which differ from retail funds in that, rather than individual investors like yourself pooling their monies, companies/institutions pool their funds in the trust, and the minimum contribution is capped at $1 million.

However, some trusts will allow you to start with amounts as little as $5, $ 10, and $50. Remember that these cheaper trusts will provide less protection on your principal, owing to their low-cost nature, and there is a higher chance of losing your money.

Unit trusts are thus an accessible way to begin building a well-diversified portfolio. It would be difficult to create a portfolio with the same level of diversification that a managed fund affords you if you invested S$1,000 on your own instead of in a UIT.

Also; if you want to rebalance the portfolio or acquire a variety of bonds or stocks while investing on your own; you will be charged a service charge, which is not something you have to worry about when investing in a unit trust.

4) Professional asset management team

Unit trusts are often run by a group of experts who will oversee the fund's portfolio and give investors access to relevant investment data, tools, and analysis.

This is a huge investment advantage compared to investing directly in the market because these professionals are usually seasoned veterans who know and understand the market well. They know which stocks and bonds to invest in and understand when the time is right to change things up in the portfolio so it does not end up "brain dead" (more of this in the potential disadvantages sub-chapter below.)

As a novice, your investments are overseen and managed at a seasoned, highly-professional level right out of the gate. This is a luxury most individual investors cannot enjoy and fall back on until they've been active investors in the market for several years.

The ability to draw on the knowledge of a group of experienced asset managers is especially advantageous for the investor who does not have much money to play with and is looking to make relatively small investments that could be easy to wipe off if invested directly in the stock market.

With the main advantages covered, let's look at the potential disadvantages of investing in these funds.

What are the Disadvantages Involved in Investing in Unit Trusts?

Here are some of the primary downsides of investing in unit trusts:

1. The fees involved

You will need to pay a fee to invest in a fund.

As we know by now, the fund manager will manage your funds and channel them to assets likely to yield returns. You will thus be required to pay the fund manager for their experience because they will be working to maximize the earnings from the investment fund.

Due to this cost, your returns can be lesser than the market. In addition, other charges like administrative fees and the like could also be necessary.

2. Liquidity constraints

We already said that unit trusts have the advantage of high liquidity, so how is it that there are liquidity constraints? Well, here's the explanation:

Typically, unit trusts use raised funds to invest in stocks or bonds in the market, with some funds opting for a mix of both.

These securities have a considerable degree of risk attached to them, owing to their sensitivity to news, not just in the market but outside, that may directly impact the companies in which these securities are held.

For instance, news that a tech company is going through a nasty split between its founders could negatively impact the value of the company's stock, which will extend to a fund investing in it. Etc.

Moreover, the news does not have to be as significant and impactful as the above example – mere rumors that make their way to the news pipeline could negatively affect the value of a company's stock, et al.

These unpredictable swings and fluctuations in stock and bond value directly impact the fund's share price. That is why it is usually best to set a unit trust investment's termination date at least three years from the fund's inception for the fund's investors to reap the benefits of investing in their preferred markets and companies.

Regardless, unit trusts have no minimum investment period, and units may be sold whenever necessary. Also, in principle, funds can terminate an investment in seven working days.

3. Minimal control of the direction of your investment

Yes, that is your money, but you have no control over it. It will be managed for you by the fund managers. You will not be able to pick precisely which stocks or bonds to invest in; these decisions are the purview of the fund manager(s).

Each unit investment trust has an objective laid out by the prospectus, as we already pointed out. As an investor, you have no say on the markets or companies (tech, healthcare, sports, et al.) that the fund invests in. That option is not available to you. You are buying into what's already there with clearly stated objectives.

As an investor, the only thing you can do as far as all this is concerned is to invest in a trust that matches your investment objectives and risk tolerance.

If your risk tolerance is higher than most, you can invest in a trust that perhaps looks to developing/niche markets or looks to have a huge capital increase by taking on more risk. If not, you can opt for trusts investing in larger, lower-risk markets with low but steady and guaranteed rewards.

4. Brain-dead portfolio

There are unit trusts referred to be 'brain-dead' portfolios. These come about when fund managers put together a portfolio for the fund but ultimately make the wrong choice in their investment choices leading to no/minimal capital growth and no/negative returns. This is what is called a brain-dead portfolio.

UITs do not have the wiggle room mutual funds have over changing the investment items in the portfolio or even conducting a full overhaul. Instead, the unit trust invests funds in what it says it will, something not subject to change.

Because of this, conducting a portfolio reconstruction process is not an option to change the fund's fortunes, as would be the case with a mutual fund.

You and your fellow investors in the fund will have to wait until the maturation period and hope you can at least get something back from your initial investment and then strike it lucky with another fund. It's easy to see why this may not be ideal.

5. Not too well-suited for short-term investments

UITs (and the same applies to their close cousins, mutual funds) are not ideal for short-term investing. We've already highlighted this fact multiple times up to this point and explained why this is the case.

As you invest your hard-earned money in a fund, understand that you cannot expect instant/quick returns like you would day trading stocks (buying stocks and holding them no longer than the duration of the trading day, which starts at 8.00 am and closes at 5.00 pm) or scalping (buying and selling stocks in the space of minutes). Not even close. It will take time to gain and require patience on your side!

UITs are a great investment, but not all investors will find them suitable. As such, before you invest in one, ensure our investment needs and preferences are congruent with the long-term investment nature of these funds.

This brings us to the next topic – who are unit trusts best suited for?

Who are Unit Trusts Most Suitable for?

Unit trusts are an excellent option for those who don't want to manage our investments personally. They are ideal for those of us who do not want to be tasked with directly deciding the assets we want to invest in.

We may not want to be directly involved in investing due to time constraints, a full plate regarding responsibilities and obligations, a lack of interest, or comprehensive knowledge of the investment market.

We may also be unwilling to pay the additional costs involved in building a personal portfolio or might be unable to make the higher minimum investment contributions necessary to invest directly in the market.

Whatever the reason, we would rather have a more experienced hand pick them for us, and we stand to benefit more from this setup.

With this said, investing in UITs may not be for everyone. Be mindful of the following before investing:

UITs do not guarantee full protection of your principal as their close cousins and mutual funds do

As such, losing your principal, or at least a sizable portion, is possible. It is best to have this in mind as you consider going in.

Do thorough introspection and make peace with the possibility of losing your principal investment amount or a sizable portion. Make sure you are comfortable with the reality that your principal is not fully protected as it would be if you invested in a mutual fund.

You must evaluate the fund's investing goal, plans, and strategy.

It is important to understand how the fund plans to reach its investment goals under various market circumstances and how in-place restrictions on the degree of risk it can incur will impact its returns.

To do this, read the fund's fact sheets and prospectuses. We have already highlighted them and even linked an example, which you can go through to get an idea of what they contain and their wording.

If you have a hard time unpacking the information in the fact sheets and prospectuses or cannot get as clear an understanding of the fund's investment goals as you would like, you can reach out to the fund manager. However, you must first go through the fact sheet before doing this.

Fund managers allow for questions and inquiries from investors. Ask them to articulate the fund's investment goal if you don't understand it in the fund prospectus. It's the investor's money and, thus, their right to know how the fund manager intends to manage it to ensure it achieves its investment goals.

Ask the fund manager(s) how they intend to invest the funds and what markets or companies they plan to channel the funds to. They may not answer you directly and may relay the information to you through an assistant, but they will email you back with the answers to your questions.

Understand the precise benchmark the fund uses and whether it aims to outperform or match the benchmark's performance.

You can do this by reviewing the fund's fact sheets and prospectuses. If you have a hard time understanding this, send the fund manager(s) an email and ask them to explain in easy-to-comprehend language what the fund benchmark is.

What is the target? What key performance indices do they have to track progress and ensure they're well on course for the goals? How often do they review the goals in place? All of this is information in the fund fact sheets and prospectuses, and you should ask and ensure you get real answers if you have difficulty deciphering these documents.

Recognize the risks associated with the fund.

Some funds use financial derivatives for investment or hedging motives. The risk of the provider (or the counterparty) of these financial derivatives defaulting is one of the risks involved in using financial derivatives that you ought to be informed about.

How diverse the fund's portfolio is, is perhaps the number one place to look when assessing the level of risk involved in investing in a fund.

The shallower and less diverse a fund is, the higher the risks involved because of the impact of possible market fluctuations. Greater diversification in the stocks and bonds in the fund's portfolio provides a better shield against devastating fluctuations and vice versa.

You will be able to know just how diverse the portfolio is by going through the fund's fact sheets and prospectuses.

Make sure you are comfortable with having your invested monies tied up for an extended period because this will certainly be the case if you invest in a UIT

Investors holding onto their investments for an extended period may manage to weather market downturns, as funds are susceptible to market fluctuations.

And with unit trusts, the deal is that they're primarily long-term investment vehicles. If you don't want your money tied down for longer, unit trusts may not be your best option.

Also, ensure you have enough financial resources before investing to avoid liquidating your assets for funds during a market crisis.

Investing in a fund might not be appropriate for you should you need to convert your investments into cash to cover urgent expenses quickly.

Next, we examine how unit trusts work and their varied investment elements.

Chapter 2: Understanding How Unit Trusts Work & Their Profitability

Unit trusts are a cheap and easy way to invest, much cheaper than going alone and investing directly in company stocks and bonds.

That is because – as mentioned – becoming a fund investor will only need you to invest a minimum sum. The professional fund manager will oversee your investment and smartly invest your money in diverse stocks and/or bonds, as laid out in the fund's fact sheets and prospectuses.

This minimum amount is typically capped at $500, albeit some funds will let you put up as little as $5.

The trust then spreads the funds over different kinds of stocks and/or bonds in a way that would have been much harder and costlier to achieve had you decided to go solo in your investment journey.

The fund manager overseeing your fund will lean on their knowledge and experience to ensure the fund only invests in the most viable stocks and/or bonds.

The manager will identify the stocks and bonds with the greatest potential for the highest yields and assemble a solid investment portfolio. They will also put together a solid investment plan and clearly define the goals and objectives of the fund, all outlined in the prospectus.

With all this in mind, let's focus on how you make gains (or losses) investing in unit trusts.

How Do Investors Make Gains/Losses in Unit Trusts?

We highlighted that most unit trust funds invest in either stocks or bonds, with some investing in a mix of the two.

A fund's underlying stock/bond values will fluctuate over time based on daily fluctuations and swings in the bond and stock markets. They also depend on the swings in interest rates of these stocks and bonds.

Investors in unit trusts make returns (gains or losses) on their initial investment when the value of the trust's underlying assets, as a whole, increases (or decreases).

These profits/losses are what we call investment returns. You must note that returns do not include profits alone; they also include losses.

Returns have three elements:

1. Capital gains result from increases in asset price, resulting in profits when these assets sell for a higher price than their original purchase price.

2. The dividends paid out to shareholders by corporations. These payments could be monthly, quarterly, bi-annually, or annually.

3. Interest accrued on bonds or cash.

These three factors, all subject to taxation, affect a fund's performance (see Chapter 5, which details taxes on all three factors).

How Much Could You Lose?

The principle or capital of UITs is not guaranteed/protected, unlike mutual funds, where your principal investment is protected, and you are guaranteed to get it back, if nothing else.

In some cases, you could lose a sizeable portion of your investment. In very rare cases, you could lose everything. The fund prospectus, and fund fact sheet, will clearly outline the investing risks of your particular fund.

Fees could also lower your returns. Typically, the fees are mandatory, whether or not the fund performs well.

So, to give a straightforward answer to the question in the sub-chapter title, you could lose it all. But this, again, happens very rarely. But either way, do understand that your principal isn't bullet-proof like it would be in a mutual fund.

How Does a Unit Trust's Performance Work?

When evaluating the unit trust fund's performance, we primarily evaluate its total return (profit or loss). The higher the net profit, the better performing the fund is. The higher the net loss, the worse the fund's performance is. It is as simple as this.

A fund's total returns consist of capital gains or losses and the fund's income distributions. Income distributions come in the form of dividends paid to you and your fellow investors, the interest rate, and the total REIT income.

Below is the formula for calculating a unit trust's total return:

Total Return = Capital Loss/Gain + Income Distribution

Units or shares in a trust can be bought or sold at any time of the day. We've also highlighted that a fund's shares are only priced once daily, which does not fluctuate for the rest of the day.

A unit trust fund's daily pricing usually directly impacts its overall return. Meaning; the return of the fund grows as the price goes up and decreases as the price goes down.

Please note that when the UIT share price drops from one day to the next, this return loss is merely a "paper loss." That means the loss is only visible on paper. If you sell your fund's units at that day's lower price, it only gets locked in (changes from being a paper loss to a "true loss").

Thus, let your investment sit for an extended period— which you should be doing anyway since investing in a UIT is meant to be a long-term investment. When you do this, you can expect the unit prices to gradually readjust from one day to the next and hopefully keep climbing as the days, weeks, and months go by.

Hence, these are called "paper losses" and not real losses unless you sell at a low price. This also explains why your chances of making a solid investment increase the longer you can keep your money invested.

Let's understand how unit trust pricing works.

How are Unit Trusts Priced?

We get the price per unit by dividing the fund's net asset value (NAV) by the total number of outstanding shares/units in the unit trust. The net asset value, or NAV, is the market value of the shares in the trust on that particular day, less the expenses incurred running the unit trust.

NAV calculation is typically daily and often done to account for fluctuations in the market prices of those assets and investments that the fund owns.

There are two different pricing structures when calculating the price per unit of a fund: bid and offer pricing and single pricing.

We'll start with the bid and offer pricing structure.

1) Bid and offer pricing

The subscription fee is added to the NAV with bid and offer pricing. This is the fee the fund manager charges for managing the fund. It typically ranges from 0.2%-2.0% per year, depending on the type of fund.

The **redemption** fee (the fee charged to the investor after a fund sells shares) gets subtracted from the figure obtained from adding the subscription fee to the NAV and then dividing this figure by the total outstanding units/shares in the fund. That is how the final price is arrived at.

Below is a description of the individual phrases:

- ✓ Bid – This is the price at which investors sell off their units

- ✓ Offer – This is the price at which the investors purchase units

- ✓ Spread – This is the difference (the spread) between the bid-and-offer prices of a fund's units. It reflects the subscription (sales) and redemption charges (if there are any).

Let's now look at single pricing.

2) Single pricing

Single pricing is a more straightforward kind of pricing.

We arrive at this pricing by dividing the fund's net asset value (NAV), which is the market value of the shares in the trust on that particular day, by the total number of outstanding shares/units in the unit trust.

However, before the units get distributed, the investment amount is reduced by subtracting the subscription fees from the total investment amount. Any redemption fee will also get subtracted from the proceeds of the redemption.

You've probably heard of unit classes. What are they? What do they entail? The subchapter below explains the concept of unit classes in trusts.

What are the Different Unit Classes?

These are the different classes in unit trusts:

1. *Classes open to individual investors, such as yourself:*

The main ones are:

i) Class A funds: This is the standard individual investor unit class.

This is the unit class that most individual investors, such as yourself, will fall in. The minimum investment amounts are set at a very reasonable level, usually $500, although the amount can be even lower from one fund to the next.

Minimum investment amounts are low to attract as many private investors to the fund as possible, making it possible to raise the necessary capital.

ii) Class T funds: This is a special class of unit trusts that individual investors such as yourself can purchase.

Established on February 1, 2016, as the "tax-free class," investors in this unit class are protected from capital gains, interest, and dividend taxation.

T-Class takes advantage of various income types' varied tax rates. The highest rate of taxation applies to interest (and employment) income, whereas lesser rates apply to dividend and capital gain income.

However, as much as they protect you from taxation on capital gains, interest, and dividends, class T funds also charge a more varied array of costs, unlike the class A ones.

2) Classes that are open to institutional investors:

B & D Classes: This class is primarily for institutions with huge sums of money to invest, with pension funds being an example. Usually, these institutions have their minimum investment amount capped at $1 million.

A fund can have different unit classes in it. Different unit classes allow a unit trust firm to charge the varied fees that come with different unit classes on unit trust investors (companies and institutions, individuals like yourself, etc.) inside a single fund.

Each unit class has a unique fee structure and varying minimum investment requirements and is available to various categories of investors.

Explaining Income Distribution

A unit trust's income comes from the units or shares of the fund. When the value or price of these units or shares increases, the fund can sell them off at a profit, thus generating income in this way.

Distributable income" is the term used to describe this income. We call it "distributable income" since it is effectively distributed to the fund's investors and unit holders.

The fund's expenditures and costs are subtracted from the income before net income calculation. As we've covered, this net income is reached by calculating the fund's daily price per unit.

The daily unit price, which we have expounded on, comprises both a capital and an income component. We calculate the income component by dividing the fund's revenue, minus expenditures, by the total number of outstanding units. The fund's capital component is calculated by dividing the value of the fund's units or shares by the total number of outstanding units.

Unit trusts are mandated to make income declarations (we've mentioned these a couple of times in passing. A fund's income declaration may be done monthly, quarterly, bi-yearly, or yearly). When the respective amounts are paid to investors, an income declaration is made on the fund's declaration/announcement date.

You, the investor, can choose to receive your income on the declaration date, or you can choose to forego your payment and have your monies reinvested back into your fund.

In the latter scenario, you will end up owning more units in the fund, but the price per unit will be lower because the unit price has decreased due to the income disclosed. Reinvesting distributions is particularly advantageous since it takes advantage of compound interest, or growth on growth, over time.

Whether you pay or reinvest those distributions, you will be taxed.

As an investor, you should be aware that changes and fluctuations in the investment market will also impact the price of a unit and that a decline in the price following an income distribution may not always be equivalent to the distribution itself.

The daily unit price could have fallen more due to a *decrease* in the marketplace value of the fund's underlying assets, or it might have fallen less due to an *increase* in the marketplace value of the assets themselves, etc.

When you purchase units in a unit investment trust, the revenue accumulated up to that moment, as was previously discussed, is included in the cost. The income earned up to that moment is marked as sold-by-investor when you decide to sell units.

For Capital Gains Tax (CGT) reasons, the income sold would be considered a portion of your proceeds, with the purchased income included in the initial cost.

As a result, revenue counts toward a taxpayer's taxable income. It isn't eligible for capital gains tax – if reported while you, the investor, still possess the units. If you sell your units before making a declaration, the gain or loss will be considered for CGT (capital gains tax) purposes and not taxpayer-taxable income purposes.

If You Have a Change of Heart: Right to Cancel

You can change your mind and cancel within seven calendar days of making your fund investment.

Although there won't be any administrative fees associated with your purchase cancellation in this period, you could incur losses if the fund's market value has decreased since the day you purchased.

If the fund's marketplace value has increased, you will be reimbursed in full, as far as your purchase price goes, but you won't be eligible for the gain. You will have the management fee returned to you.

You cannot exercise your right to cancel if:

- ✓ You are adding to an existing fund that you currently already own

- ✓ You invested in a fund listed on the US Exchange.

You now know everything there is to know about what unit trust funds are and how they work. You're now ready to get into the investment aspect of the same. Chapter 3 looks at this.

Chapter 3: The Different Ways of Investing in a Unit Trust

The investment landscape can be – and often is – very dynamic and constantly changing.

However, investors that take time to fully comprehend the fundamental elements of investing in UITs, the different asset classes, and the different ways you can invest in a fund stand a greater chance of benefitting greatly in the long run.

This chapter looks at the different ways you can invest in unit trusts.

The Different Ways You Can Invest in a Unit Trust

There are two primary ways to invest in a unit trust – directly dealing with the unit trust firm or investing via a Linked Investment Services Provider, or LISP.

A LISP acts as a bridge between you and the unit investment trust and handles the requisite investment demands, paperwork, et al. for you. Of course, this service comes with a fee you would otherwise not pay if you decided to invest directly.

In either case, you may make your investment either directly or with the aid of an Independent Financial Advisor (IFA). An IFA will work with you to decide which kind of fund is best suited for you.

This guide goes into greater detail on each option's pros and cons/expenses.

Let's examine each one of these investment options:

Directly investing with a unit trust firm

To invest directly with a unit trust firm, you must fill out an application, present the required FICA documentation (learn more about FICA later in the chapter), and decide which fund you want to invest in.

As product suppliers, unit trust firms cannot offer you, the investor, any investment advice—this is a regulation. If you want investment advice, you have to work with an IFA. This stipulation is in place to avoid prejudice or potential conflict of interest in endorsing particular unit trusts.

You can only get investment advice from licensed investment advisors, some employed by financial services firms and others who work independently. But any unit investment trust you decide to invest with cannot offer investment advice or recommendations by law.

While investing directly may be less expensive because you won't have to pay IFA advisor fees, it's important to remember that there are (many) additional risks involved.

For starters, it will be entirely on you to pick a fund to invest in. And as a newbie, the chances of choosing the wrong fund to invest in are quite high, and it may be in your best interest to work with an advisor to pick a fund.

As a novice, we do not recommend this option, as there is so much you do not know about the investment landscape. This option is a better fit for seasoned investors who already have a feel of the market.

Investing via a Linked Investment Services Provider (LISP)

A LISP is an administrative platform accredited by the financial sector authority and is used for packaging, distributing, and managing various investment products, among other things.

The LISP will be a middleman or a bridge between you and the fund you want to invest in. They will deal with the fund on your behalf and ensure everything is ready for you to become an investor in the fund.

Although LISPs, like unit trust firms, are not authorized to provide financial advice, most LISPs will nonetheless recommend (sometimes even insist) that you consult an IFA before deciding which fund you want to invest in.

Once you've worked with an IFA to pinpoint the best fund for you, the LISP will navigate the registration process so you can invest in the fund. All you need do is avail your FICA documents and any documents and details they may require; they will handle the rest and charge a fee for their services.

Speaking of FICA documentation, let's explore what it is and what it entails.

What is FICA & Why Is It Relevant?

The Financial Intelligence Centre Act (FICA) was approved in 2001. Its role is to prevent money laundering, which is the misuse of financial systems to conceal the proceeds of crime and other unsavory financial activities such as terrorism funding.

The FICA Act mandates that financial institutions ensure they have all their clients' accurate information before allowing them to invest with them. Owing to this, new clients and investors must provide evidence to prove their identity, banking information, physical address, and income tax details.

In addition to authenticating the identity of investors investing with them, FICA requires financial institutions to authenticate any investment professionals or entities who may be acting on their behalf.

This is mandated to determine their investment profile and weed out any alleged or suspicious activity. If the FICA standards are not adhered to, accountable establishments have the right to refuse or promptly end business partnerships or transactions without any ramifications.

What details do you need to provide?

The following FICA-mandated information is required when you request to join a trust or engage in any other type of financial transaction:

1) A legible copy of a recent utility bill with your name and real address (not a PO Box), no older than 3 months

2) Your social security details along with income tax ID details

3) A recent (no more than 3 months old) bank statement with your name and account number. You must provide proof of transaction if your funds are not taken electronically/digitally from your savings account.

You must make sure your FICA documentation is promptly updated. If your contact information changes, you must inform the relevant accountable FICA personnel to update your details in the FICA system. Doing this is easier when working with a LISP, as they will do everything for you.

With an understanding of FICA documentation, why it is compulsory, and what you must provide, we can now move on to how much you should invest in a unit investment trust.

How Much Should You Invest in a Unit Trust?

You already know how much you *can* invest in a unit trust, as we've already covered the minimum investment amounts for retail investors.

But this begs the question – how much *should* you invest in one? The answer to this is pretty simple – only invest as much money as you're comfortable parting with for an extended period.

As we have highlighted time and time again, a unit investment trust is not the ideal investment vehicle to direct funds that you know you will need in a short period. Only invest funds that you won't need for a while.

Is a Debit Order a Smarter Choice than a Lump Sum Investment and Vice Versa?

You can invest one-time or perhaps even non-periodic sums of money— a lump sum —into a unit trust fund or make smaller, regular contributions via a periodic debit order.

But which one is the better option?

Regular, periodic investing, aka periodic debit orders, have the advantage of forming and ingraining a healthy habit of putting money aside and making savings. And with the amounts being significantly less than the lump sum, they will be less noticeable when you take them off your paycheck and direct them to your fund capital investment.

Thus, it is the superior option, especially for the beginner investor who may not have much money to invest and needs time to put together their capital investment.

Another advantage is that if you commit to a periodic debit order but can no longer afford your regular monthly investment amount, you can legally discontinue your periodic investment without paying fees for discontinuing your periodic investment.

However, each fund varies from the next. As such, review your fund's fact sheets and prospectus and see if they attach any charges to discontinuing debit orders.

With this said, you need to be truly honest with yourself. Are you incapable of making your debit order now, or do you have other non-basic and non-emergency things you want to spend it on? Strive to avoid using any justification to halt your routine debit order because doing so will prevent you from achieving your investment objectives.

Next up, we look at assets, risks, and returns.

Chapter 4: All About Unit Trust Assets, Risk, Returns, and Volatility

This chapter covers the following:

- ✓ The various asset classes and how they produce returns.

- ✓ Risk, return, and volatility and the relationship between them.

- ✓ Why your UIT returns must return trump inflation.

We'll start with the varied asset classes and how they produce returns.

What are the Different Asset Classes, and How Do They Produce Returns?

1) Equity

Stock or equity will represent a share or slice of ownership in a company. UITs invest in company stock, among other assets.

The value of a company's stock depends on numerous factors and fluctuations (rises or falls) over time. These fluctuations reflect in the share or unit price of the fund, producing either gains or losses for the shareholders/investors. In addition, companies might pay dividends to their shareholders, representing a slice of the company's yearly profits.

Generally, dividends are paid out every 6 months and can provide a steady income for investors. Historically, equities have produced the highest returns over time for investors, making them an ideal investment class for UITs. However – and we have already touched on this – they represent considerable risk. This is because: -

1) As previously discussed, they are highly sensitive to news and rumors.

2) Share prices are subject to big daily market movements. This is called "volatility," or the movement degree over time.

The higher a stock's volatility is, the higher the associated risk. Similarly, UITs that only invest in equities are usually at a higher risk than those that invest in other assets.

Volatility decreases the longer the investment period is. And the longer a UIT stays invested in equities, the less risky they become since the probability of incurring losses diminishes over time. These are reasons why UITs are primarily long-term investment vehicles.

2) Listed property

Some unit trusts invest in property companies listed on the stock market.

This exposes them to various assets, including office, commercial, industrial, and residential properties. A listed property company's share offers returns via the rise or drop in the share price. This results in capital gains/losses.

Additionally, it provides income in the shape of periodic shareholder distributions on the rental fees and income these companies earn. This income is often very closely linked to inflation. This element provides a key distinction to other equities, where dividends are not quite as steady/reliable over time as those of listed property companies.

This distinction makes investing in the stocks of listed property companies considerably less risky than other equities, as their distributions have a higher chance of being steadier. This also gives listed properties the traits of both equities and bonds.

Listed property values, generally, behave quite differently to other equities in similar conditions on the market, making this asset class an awesome diversifier for UITs. Concerning investing in this asset class, fund managers primarily prefer to invest in Real Estate Investment Trusts, or REITs.

A REIT is a listed property company governed by very strict regulations regarding its operations and structure. These regulations also mostly favor the investor over the company. For instance, REITs must pay their shareholders at least 75% of all distributable profits. This explains why they are attractive investment options for UITs.

3) Bonds & Credit Instruments/Items

Bonds and other credit instruments are company/government loans.

Some funds will primarily focus on bonds issued by companies (corporate bonds.) Others will prefer to invest in bonds offered by the government (government bonds.) In both cases, bondholders lend their money to the entity (the company or government). In return, they get regular interest payments and a final repayment sum after a specified time. This is typically a year or more but rarely less than a year.

The fund earns interest as a regular income paid to you and your fellow investors. The fund also repays its initial investment sum when the bond term ends.

Generally, bonds are less risky assets when compared to equities. The reason for this is because, should they have financial difficulties, companies must pay their bondholders before they even pay their shareholders.

Historically, bond yields and prices have not been prone to big swings and fluctuations like equities have, making them less volatile and risky investments.

4) Cash

Cash, and other equivalent assets, are securities embodying the form of short-term loans that earn regular interest, usually with a repayment term of less than a year.

These can comprise an array of money market items such as bankers' assurances, certificates of deposit, promissory notes, and commercial company paper.

Given their shorter maturation period compared to bonds, the interest payments made, and thus the return to investors, are typically lower than bonds. Nevertheless, they also present a lower investment risk than bonds owing to this shorter repayment period.

Generally, these are the lowest-risk investment type that UITs can make, other than actual cash/banknote holdings.

However, there is a real chance they can lose value in a financial crisis, should banks, or other issuers, be unable to repay their debts in full.

5) Offshore Assets

Equities, bonds, property, and cash not listed in the US are regarded as offshore assets.

Because they are usually varied in foreign currency, they carry an added currency risk that could negatively impact the investment value (should the US dollar appreciate against the investment's currency) or positively (should the US dollar depreciate against the investment's currency.)

Thus far, we have touched on risk, volatility, and returns multiple times associated with the different asset classes covered.

Below, we will explain risk, return, and volatility in UITs and their relationship.

A Guide to Understanding Risk, Return & Volatility in Unit Investment Trusts

This guide aims to help you better understand the link between risk, return, and volatility.

It will also provide helpful advice to help you understand your risk tolerance and, perhaps, aid you in making smarter investing choices regarding choosing the right investment fund.

Risk and return have an inextricable link in everything you do. The same applies to investing.

You take hundreds of risks daily, even while you might not give risk much thought. You take risks when driving to work, showering, or deciding what to eat for lunch or dinner.

Often, these are "calculated" risks you have chosen to take after carefully evaluating the circumstances and your available options. For instance, you take the risk of driving to work because if you don't and decide to take the safer option of walking or commuting, the chances of arriving late at work are higher. These daily risks that we take only become significant when something goes wrong.

The "Global Financial Crisis" of 2008 is perhaps the best illustration of what happens when the concept of risk does not attract the seriousness it mandates:

Financial institutions worldwide invested in significantly riskier assets – much riskier in numerous cases than initially presented— to maximize returns. They presented the value of the assets they invested in lower than what they were being purchased and sold for. Ultimately, the ravages of these decisions were of an epic level, and millions of people lost homes and livelihoods in hours.

It was an extremely harsh lesson that if your calculations are off, taking calculated risks, or what you think are calculated risks, can have disastrous results.

Our Definition of 'Risk' when Investing in Funds

There are many ways to define risk, but to keep things straightforward, let's evaluate investment risk in three ways: -

1. You could end up losing some/all of your initial investment

When you invest in a trust fund, you ideally want the investments the fund makes to appreciate and eventually be resold for a profit, thereby raising the unit/share value and providing returns on your investment.

However, there is no absolute assurance that this will happen. Any investment you make could lose some or all of its value. This is especially true when investing in UITs, where your principal investment is not protected.

There is no absolute certainty that your investment will perform as your fund's asset manager anticipates, even if its value grows.

2. Your investment could be less valuable in the future than it is now

It's important to remember that inflation, the increase in necessities like food and shelter, might eventually reduce the investment's value.

If, for example, an investment yields 1.5% annually, but yearly inflation is 2%, your invested amounts will certainly be worth less when you decide to take it out/spend it. And since very low-interest rates have decreased the rewards available via cash savings accounts, this "inflation risk" has been more of an issue lately than it was in the past.

3. Your investment journey could be markedly uncomfortable

Investing returns can indeed be unpredictable, and this is especially true for riskier investments.

However, if you (or, in this case, the fund you're investing in) takes fewer risks when putting together an investment portfolio, your investment journey will likely be more comfortable, and the returns will be steadier and more guaranteed. Still, it can take much longer to get to your investment goals.

Putting risk into context

The primary risk for the majority of investors is losing money.

The risk of losing money is always there, particularly when dealing with individual stocks and even bonds, which UITs primarily invest in. Still, funds also practice portfolio diversification which helps lower that risk.

Your fund spreading its investments will give it more control over the risks and predicted return on investment.

Generating steady returns while remaining within reasonable risk levels is the foundation for a fund's sustained performance. Your fund's asset manager must strike the right balance when assembling a fund's portfolio.

The Relationship Between Risk and Return

The ultimate goal of every fund is to generate returns on its investment. The assets, typically stocks and bonds, must generate adequate returns to accomplish the fund's – and thus its investors – long-term objectives.

But to get there, a fund manager must take certain essential risks:

1) Risk & return go together

Without addressing risk, having a rational conversation about investment is impossible.

Every fund wants the best returns on its investment.

But if an investment fund guarantees high returns without disclosing the risks, it will take or intends to take your money; it is undoubtedly too good to be true.

2) Making a Choice Between Lower or Higher Risk Investments

One of the fundamental investing principles is that higher-risk investments should, in theory, result in greater rewards. But in the investment world, there certainly are no guarantees.

High-risk, high-reward investments are just that – the risks are high, but the *potential* rewards are high. The key word here is 'potential.'

A fund investing in a niche market or a developing market/industry without a considerable performance footprint to evaluate could lose its investment altogether. However, if all goes right, the fund could see huge rewards that it otherwise wouldn't have had its portfolio built around low-risk assets.

A very low-risk investment, on the other hand, with the example of putting your funds in a personal savings account, will not produce much in the way of returns. Your return is pretty much guaranteed, but it's very low. Moreover, this minimal return could even fail to outpace inflation. That represents the other end of the spectrum of risk.

There is no "one size fits all" solution regarding the level of risk that a fund, and its investors, are willing to face. Some funds prioritize minimizing loss and guaranteeing steady if unspectacular returns, so they build their portfolio around low-risk, low-reward assets.

Some funds prioritize huge capital gains growth and will risk more of their money in exchange for the possibility of earning significantly higher returns.

The majority of funds, however, fall somewhere in the middle, willing to face certain financial risks but willing to forego the chance of larger returns by making investments that reduce their risk of experiencing capital losses.

Assembling the proper mix of fund investments to satisfy these different needs and creating portfolios intended to produce the greatest return for the necessary degree of risk is therefore crucial.

Volatility Explained

When choosing the best assets, your fund manager must properly understand volatility. You, the investor, must properly understand the same so you're smarter when choosing the fund to invest in.

The problem is that there aren't many in-depth discussions on volatility, especially when investing in UITs.

Volatility is a method for estimating the risk of a specific investment over a predetermined time frame. An investment with high volatility is more likely to undergo frequent, possibly significant, price swings than one with low volatility.

1) Measuring Volatility

"Standard deviation" is the most widely used metric for measuring volatility.

This metric calculates how much an investment's returns depart from its average returns. Investments with higher volatility vary from the average with more frequency than those with low volatility.

Volatility is also expressed as a percentage, similar to how investment returns are displayed.

Consider an investment with a history of annualized volatility of 10% and a 7% average yearly return over the previous ten years.

Going by these figures, the spectrum of returns during the past ten years has, for little over two-thirds of the period (there is a variance of +/- 10% above the average return allowed), ranged between 17% and -3%. The returns fell outside of this range for one-third of the time.

2) Managing Volatility

To target particular degrees of risk, fund managers may use the estimates of the volatility of various kinds of assets they want to invest in when putting together portfolios.

This strategy, known as "risk targeting," increases the likelihood that a fund's investment portfolio will perform as anticipated, even though it is difficult to predict with precision what the yield and volatility of the investment will be as time goes by.

The majority of funds, however, do not prioritize minimizing volatility. They usually aim to maximize the returns on the assets they invest in. Typically, this entails attempting to beat the benchmark for their sector.

As a result, the level of risk inside a fund can vary considerably, even for funds in the same sector, and the volatility is exceedingly difficult to forecast.

3) Volatility and Time

Your fund's investment time frame may significantly impact its portfolio performance.

The impact of an investment's volatility is lessened if you intend to hold it for a long period. The market's swings and rallies become far less meaningful if invested for a considerable time.

The possible swings are far more obvious and are likelier to have a greater impact on returns when investing for shorter periods.

Why is It So Vital that Your Returns Trump Inflation?

Inflation may be defined as climbing prices over a while, and it essentially shows how rapidly living expenses are rising.

Your investment will lose value over time due to inflation, and so to preserve its worth, it must grow at least as fast as inflation. It should, ideally, grow faster than inflation. For this reason, many unit trust funds deliberately aim for growth that exceeds inflation when putting together their portfolio.

The higher the targeted rate above inflation, the fund must assume more risk. It is crucial to remember that owing to the short-term nature of their assets, even the lowest-risk unit trusts, such as money market funds, may be unable to generate returns over inflation. As an investor, you should know this significant risk when choosing which fund to invest in.

With the different asset classes covered and the relationship between risk, volatility, and returns covered, the next step is to cover the costs involved in investing in UITs.

The next chapter will examine the assorted costs, fees, charges, and taxes involved in fund investment and how they affect you.

Chapter 5: A Comprehensive Guide on the Costs Involved in Investing in Unit Trusts

This chapter looks at the different costs involved in investing in UITs.

Investing in UITs involves various fees, whether directly through a unit trust firm or indirectly, via a linked investment services provider (LISP) and/or with an IFA.

All service providers have a legal obligation to disclose their charges to investors, and they typically mention these obligations in their marketing materials. All service fees covered here do not include the additional 15% VAT tax. However, the fees and expenses are scheduled and regulated.

Let's get into it.

We'll start with the varied charges levied and then move on to taxes.

1) Total Expense Ratio (TER)

The TER is helpful when comparing the expenses of investing in various unit trusts since it quantifies the direct gross costs associated with administering a unit trust. It is a transparent metric that all fund management firms regularly publish for every one of their funds.

The TER covers expenses for management, trustee, legal, audit, and other operational costs. It is a portion/percentage of the portfolio's mean net asset value (NAV).

Remember that neither a low nor a high TER necessarily indicates a good or poor return. Future TERs cannot also be accurately predicted based on the existing TER. It is also crucial to remember that the TER frequently excludes costs levied by an IFA or a LISP platform.

It is also necessary to mention transaction costs and the total investment charge when discussing TER and how they relate.

Transaction Cost (TC) measures the expenses related to purchasing and selling the underlying assets in a fund. Total Investment Charge (TIC) is the sum of a fund's TER and TC.

2) Initial Fees

Initial fees may apply when purchasing units in a new investment, whether with a lump sum, top-up, or debit order.

Initial fees get subtracted from the total amount invested in the fund before investing.

The real/true investment will thus be less than the initial investment due to this subtraction. Let's touch on the initial fees you can expect to pay.

a) Your Fund's Initial Fees

Most funds do not charge initial fees. However, the fee is often negotiable with those that do and will be no higher than 3%.

b) Financial Adviser (IFA) Initial Fees

If you work with an IFA when choosing the ideal investment fund, the maximum they can charge is 3% of the investment.

Some IFAs prefer to scrap the initial fee altogether, favoring a greater ongoing fee.

c) LISP Initial Fees

The majority of LISPs will not charge initial fees. The few who charge them will not ask for over 3% of your investment.

3) Annual Fees

a) Annual Fees Charged by the Unit Investment Trust Company

The unit trust firm charges this continuing annual management fee in exchange for managing the fund and overseeing the investments. These fees will differ from one fund to the next, and there is no specific stipulation as far as they are concerned.

b) Annual Fees Charged by the IFA

Usually, these fees apply when an investor sells their fund unit. This charge is directly negotiable with your IFA and agreed to in advance because investors have direct contracts with their IFAs.

c) Annual Fees Charged by the LISP platform

Several fee structures apply from one LISP platform to the next. Your LISP, should you choose to work with one, will outline all the necessary annual fee details. But generally, your LISP will charge platform fees to cover their services.

They will effectively act as a bridge between you and the fund you want to invest in, saving you all the hassle that would otherwise be necessary without this bridge.

The financial sector is currently moving toward "clean-priced" funds: a clear price structure separates the various fees that may apply. Under clean pricing, the fees for a unit trust firm are paid directly to the fund, the administrator receives the administration fees, the financial adviser receives their advisory fees, and the LISP receives their service provision fees.

Let's move on to fund-switching fees.

4) Switching Fees

These fees may apply if you switch from one fund to another, whether in the same unit trust management firm or a different one.

Most companies will not charge switching fees if you switch between funds under their umbrella. However, most management firms and investment platforms will charge a fixed fee for every switch you make to funds under a different management company's umbrella.

5) Exit Fees

This charge, which depends on the initial capital deposited and the fund's development, may be incurred if you liquidate your investment within a specific time frame (for example, within the first year). Exit fees are not common among fund management organizations, but certain management firms have them.

This charge, dependent on the initial capital deposited in addition to the fund's development, may be incurred if you sell your investment within a specific time frame (for example, within the first year).

6) Performance Fees

The asset managers of some unit trusts impose performance-based charges correlated with the success of the fund's performance. A performance fee can apply if a fund performs better than its benchmark.

You're now familiar with the different fees involved in investing in a UIT.

Next up, we look at fund taxes.

Are Unit Investment Trusts Taxable?

They are, indeed. Any income distributions and capital gains from investments in unit trusts may be liable to the USA's income tax or capital gains tax.

The type of share class you choose and the revenue or capital appreciation you have earned will determine how much tax you may ultimately owe.

How is Income Tax Paid on Unit Trusts?

Any income distributions you get from your investment are subject to taxation. For taxation purposes, the income will continue accruing to you even if you decide to reinvest the unit trust's regular payouts. You must keep this in mind.

The composition of the fund's underlying assets (stocks, bonds, or other assets) determines whether a fund investor receives a dividend or interest payments. That will also determine the amount of income tax possibly owed.

After each tax year, the management company for your unit trust will send you a tax certificate outlining all the local and international interest, dividends, and REIT income you have earned.

All income distributions will be classified as interest payments if cash or interest-bearing assets (such as gilts or government bonds) make up upwards of 60% of the fund's underlying investments. Any income distributions are considered dividends if this is less than 60%.

The good news is that if you get dividend payments, you are entitled to a $2,500 dividend allowance (current tax year:

2022/23). As a result, all income received that falls under this amount will be taxed at 0%. Above this amount, however, dividend income is liable to taxation as follows:

- 7.7% (for basic-rate taxpayers)
- 32.0% (for higher-rate taxpayers)
- 38.2% (for additional-rate taxpayers)

The first $6,000 of income distributions received as interest may be taxed at 0% (starting rate for investments in the current tax year: 2021/22) if paid out to you grossly and recognized as savings income.

This rate allowance does not apply to anyone making more than $20,500 because it is reduced by $1 for every $1 you make in non-savings earnings over your allowance, presently $14,570.

However, basic-rate taxpayers may use their $1000 in tax-free personal savings (current tax year). For higher-rate taxpayers, this drops to $500, while additional-rate taxpayers pay nothing. Overpayments of income distributions will be subject to the following taxation metrics:

- 22% (basic-rate taxpayers)
- 42% (for higher-rate taxpayers)
- 47% (for additional-rate taxpayers)

Capital Gains Tax

Once you decide to sell units/shares from your unit trust, it will promptly trigger capital gains if their value has improved since you made your investment.

Unit trusts use the Weighted Average Base Cost method to calculate CGT. A capital gain is a difference between the base cost and the figure at the time of money withdrawal or disinvestment (or even a capital loss if the unit value has deteriorated).

You must pay taxes on capital gains in the particular tax year you sell your shares/units. Any capital gain is annually excluded from individual taxes. A tax certificate will be sent to you after each tax year, whether you've made a capital gain/loss on your investment.

Calculating capital gains tax on unit trusts – examples

Your income tax bracket, determined by your taxable income and any capital gains beyond your tax-free allowance, determines the rate used to determine the total amount of capital gains tax, or CGT, you are liable for.

If your income falls within this range, you will be subject to a 10% capital gains tax on any gains. You will be required to pay 20% for higher rates and additional rates.

For instance, if taxable returns are $25,000, and the total capital gains after deducting the tax-free allowance are $600, your total earnings would fall below the basic-rate level ($40,000 in the current tax year). Therefore you would only owe $60 in CGT/capital gains tax (10 percent) on your gains.

But, if the total taxable income exceeded $40,000, you would fall inside the higher-rate level and be subject to a 20% tax charge on any capital gains that exceeded your tax-free limit. In the scenario above, this would entail a tax charge of $120.

Will there be any CGT implications if I switch from one fund to another?

When you move from one fund to the next, regardless of whether you are switching to a fund under the same fund management umbrella or to one under a different management firm, you will be selling units from one fund and purchasing units from another fund. Hence you will be liable for CGT implications.

Avoid switching funds too frequently, as it can diminish returns.

Speaking to a financial expert

This may be unnecessary, especially because the fund fact sheet and prospectus outline everything you need to know about your fund's charges and taxes.

Nevertheless, liaising with a financial expert won't hurt, especially if you have difficulty comprehending the varied charges and taxes outlined in the fact sheet and prospectus.

A financial expert will help you better understand how your fund, and other similar funds in your unit class, work when it comes to taxation. It is also a brilliant idea to engage the services of a financial expert before deciding which fund to invest in.

The good news is that you can kill two birds with one stone here. If you engage the services of an IFA before making your fund pick (we've covered what IFAs do in-depth already), you may also receive tax-related advice.

Conclusion

Unit trusts, or UITs, are amazing investment options. They offer diversification and expert channeling of your investment by your fund manager to the most viable assets. These are things you otherwise wouldn't be able to enjoy and fall back on if you chose to trade directly in the market or would otherwise need much money for.

While UITs are straightforward enough investment options, it still helps to know as much about them as possible, which this guide should help you with. The better informed you are, the smarter your choices. And in the investment world, smarter choices are closely linked with better returns and fewer losses.

So, use the contents of this guide to pick the absolute best fund for you so that when all is said and done, you will be able to meet all your investment goals and be proud of your journey.

PS: I'd like your feedback. If you are happy with this book, please leave a review on Amazon.

Please leave a review for this book on Amazon by visiting the page below:

https://amzn.to/2VMR5qr

Printed in Great Britain
by Amazon